A Frog book
Published in 1989 by
W.H. Allen & Co Plc
Sekforde House
175/9 St John St
London EC1V 4LL

Designed and Art Directed by Susan Mann
Story adaptation by Neil and Ting Morris

Produced by the Justin Knowles Publishing Group
9 Colleton Crescent, Exeter, Devon

Printed in the U.K.

ISBN 1-85556-005-4

Robin Hood

Illustrated by Mary Kuper

Retold by Neil and Ting Morris

Designed and Art Directed by Susan Mann

CHILDREN'S CLASSICS

FROG

A long time ago there lived a band of outlaws
in Sherwood Forest, and their leader was Robin Hood.
Robin was the best archer in the land,
but he had been driven outside the law
by the greedy Prince John and his sheriffs,
who ruled the country.
The Sheriff of Nottingham was the cruellest of men.
He taxed the people so heavily
that many families starved to death.
He also killed anyone caught in the forest hunting for food.
But Robin was never too far away to help his friends.

Sherwood Forest became the hom
of many brave and honest men.
Anyone who wanted to join the band
had to live by Robin's rules.
"Never rob the poor or the old,
and never harm any woman or child,
Robin told his friends.
"My plan is not to kill the rich,
but to bring them here to dine

and let them pay
for our service.
We'll charge a high price
and share the money with the poor.
Never forget these rules,
so that one day when King Richard
returns from the Crusades,
I can proudly say, 'It was not
we who broke the law,
but your brother,
Prince John.'"

Rich lords no longer dared
to travel through Sherwood Forest,
for fear of having to join Robin's table
and dine with Will Scarlet,
Little John and the others.
None of them enjoyed listening
to Alan a Dale the minstrel's songs,
or saying grace with Friar Tuck.

But the outlaws loved entertaining their guests,
and the person they most longed to welcome
was the Sheriff of Nottingham.
It was worth waiting for him.

From their hiding place Robin and Little John watched the Sheriff and his guards, who were on their way to deliver taxes to Prince John.
"Welcome, Sheriff, to our humble home,"
Robin shouted in greeting.
"Soon you shall dine,
but first let us help you unload
the gold you stole from the poor."
"Never!" the Sheriff shouted back,
but a hail of arrows silenced him.
"I'll get my revenge for this,"
he muttered to himself,
as the outlaws
took all the money.

The Sheriff almost choked on his dinn
and only ate for fear of what
the outlaws would otherwise do to him.
But as soon as he was released,
he ordered his men
to burn down Robin's home village
and capture his great friend,
Maid Marian. He planned
to use her as bait to lure Robin
out of the forest.
But Marian had been warned.

When they
were children,
Robin had taught her
how to use a bow
and arrow,
so that one day
she could join his band.
Now that day had come.
Dressed in her brother's clothes,
she left to find
the outlaws' secret valley.

In Sherwood Forest Robin met a stranger
carrying a longbow.
"What brings you here?"
Robin asked, barring the way.
"What I do is none of your business,"
the stranger snapped.
But Robin stood his ground.
"You are in outlaw country,"
he said, "and I make
your business mine."

"Then take me to your leader," the stranger demanded, "for I've come to join his band of archers." The stranger took aim and shot a distant bird without hesitation.

"Who taught you, young man?" Robin asked.

"I am *your* pupil, Robin Hood," laughed the stranger, taking off her cap. It was Maid Marian!

Now Maid Marian was an outlaw too,
and she was a fearless companion to Robin and his men.
She bravely took up their fight for justice,
and gave the money they collected to the poor.
At dusk she often slipped into Nottingham
to find out the latest news.
In this way Robin always knew
when to expect a knight
or rich bishop in Sherwood Forest.

One cold winter's day the outlaw
held up a knight in shabby ar
"I am Sir Richard," the knight said,
"and you won't find me worth robbing."
He explained to Robin that after Prince Jo
had thrown his son into prison,

he had pledged his land and castle
to a rich abbot to buy his son's freedom.
"You should have come to us if you
wanted justice," Robin told him.
Then he gave him a bag of gold.
"That should pay your debts,"
Robin said. "Tell your abbot
that the prince of the outlaws
sends his greetings."
Sir Richard vowed
that he would repay Robin
for his kindness.

All the time the Sheriff of Nottingham was planning his revenge. He offered many rewards, but no one could capture the great outlaw. The Sheriff knew that Robin and his men were proud archers, and so he arranged a special competition.

The prize for the winner was a silver arrow. Messengers went all around the country announcing the great contest,

and the Sheriff made doubly sure
that the news reached Sherwood Forest.
On the appointed day Robin said to his friends,
"I must win the silver arrow,
but we must disguise ourselves
in order to remain unknown."

All the lords and ladies came to watch the archers.
Robin was disguised as an old man,
and the crowd booed as he stood at the mark.
But when the Sheriff saw the old man's arrow
smack into the bull's eye,
he knew the bowman could be none other
than his arch enemy, Robin Hood.
"It's Hood, the traitor!" the Sheriff shouted.
"After him!" At once his guards chased Robin and his friends.
The outlaws fought bravely,
but were outnumbered and almost overpowered.

Watching the battle from his castle,
Sir Richard saw the Sheriff's men were gaining ground.
He quickly lowered the drawbridge
and let the outlaws into his castle.
The Sheriff and his guards
returned to Nottingham empty-handed.
Robin thanked Sir Richard for his help,
and after great celebration
the outlaws slipped back to Sherwood Forest
under cover of darkness.

But Robin
could not rest.
He wandered
through the dark forest
thinking about the injustice
they all had to suffer,
when a knight
rode up to him.
As the knight
came closer,
Robin recognized him
and fell to his knees.
It was indeed King Richard
returned from the Crusade
Robin explained
to his monarch
how honest men

had been forced
to live as outlaws.
The king was horrified.
"You and your men
are free
from this hour,"
he said.
"My brother
and his sheriffs
shall have no more power
in this land."
Robin thanked King Richard,
and vowed
to continue
to serve him
and the cause
of justice forever.